CELLO

D1229037

My Very Best Christmas

17 Cello Solos, Duets and a play-along audio on Christmas favorites

Piano Accompaniment Included
Great for Suzuki groups

Arranged and Edited
by Karén Khanagov

Online Audio   www.melbay.com/99922BCDEB

AUDIO CONTENTS

1 Joy to the World [1:46]	10 What Child is This? [1:38]
2 O Come, All Ye Faithful [1:56]	11 Angels We Have Heard on High [1:58]
3 Deck the Halls [1:11]	12 Silent Night [3:00]
4 Angels from the Realms of Glory [1:29]	13 O Little Town of Bethlehem [2:19]
5 Away in a Manger [2:20]	14 We Three Kings [1:51]
6 Infant Holy, Infant Lowly [2:02]	15 O Holy Night [2:10]
7 Hark, the Herald Angels Sing [2:00]	16 Jingle Bells [1:47]
8 It Came Upon a Midnight Clear [2:28]	17 We Wish You a Merry Christmas [:47]
9 The First Noel [2:15]	

Performed, recorded and produced by Karén Khanagov at HANAGA Records.
Assistant engineer German Khanagov

Page 39 is left blank intentionally.

1 2 3 4 5 6 7 8 9 0

Visit us on the Web at www.melbay.com — E-mail us at email@melbay.com

Contents

Introduction

Hello, Young Musician!

I hope you are getting into the Christmas mood with *My Very Best Christmas*.

The songs in this volume, arranged in comfortable keys, can be used for players at different levels and for all kinds of occasions.

I loved playing the accompaniment audio. It was a lot of fun, whether I tried to play with good tone, vibrato, expressions, making up new lines or just playing beautiful tunes one after another. I improvised duets by ear with my son German. My Suzuki group played it numerous times during the holiday seasons. All of us had so much fun that we decided to share this joyful feeling with you.

If you are a beginner, you will find it fairly easy to play the melody and follow the lead of the piano. If you are an advanced player, you can transfer melodies an octave up, or add some notes and runs.

The audio can also be used for easy listening or as a solid backup for experimental variations-improvisations. You may ask, "Me? Improvise?" Why not? Musicians who can improvise began one day just as you are now, developing the skill over the years. Give it a try; you may like what you hear. It may set your mind free to create your own music.

Listening to the audio prior to playing is important for young children. At bedtime, mom or dad can sing in a soft voice to them with audio accompaniment, something they will remember for the rest of their lives. Singing together as a group is another joyful Christmas experience.

As you see, there are many things you can do with this audio and music. If you have an accompanist you can use the piano accompaniment book. In all, remember that music is a living spirit, not printed information on a music staff. A performer's goal should be to release the spirit of the music to those who listen. Right notes, rhythms, bowings, tone, and etc. are only helpers in your expressions. Make music live!

Christmas has a spirit of giving. Christ was given to us. We rejoice about it with gifts for others that represent our love. You give listeners the very special gift of your beautiful playing. The more you give the happier it makes you feel. Giving the gift of music can turn this Christmas into *Your Very Best Christmas*.

Your Friend,
Karén Khanagov

Joy to the World

George Frederick Handel

O Come, All Ye Faithful

2.

John Francis Wade

Deck the Halls

3.

Traditional

9

Angels from the Realms of Glory

4.

Henry Smart

Away in a Manger

5.

James Murray
William Kirkpatrick

Infant Holy, Infant Lowly

6.

Traditional Polish Carol

Hark, the Herald Angels Sing

7.

Felix Mendelson

It Came Upon a Midnight Clear

8.

Richard S. Willis

The First Noel

9.

Traditional English carol

slower

rit.

rit.

What Child is This?

10.

English Traditional

23

Angels We Have Heard on High

11.

Traditional

Silent Night

12.

Franz Gruber

O Little Town of Bethlehem

13.

Lewis H.Redner

We Three Kings

14.

John H. Hopkins, Jr.

O Holy Night

15.

Adolphe Adam

Jingle Bells

16.

J. Pierpont

35

We Wish You a Merry Christmas

17.

Traditional

Karén Khanagov

Karén Khanagov, Armenian by origin was born in Baku, Russia. Demanding Russian teachers and the influence of J. Heifitz, D. Oistrach and L. Kogan formed his high musical standards. His most recent work in Russia, for the Azerbaijan State Orchestra "Gaya," included combined positions of solo/orchestra performer, arranger and musical director. After becoming a refugee and settling in Oklahoma City, he began intensive violin teaching, mixing both traditional Russian and Suzuki methods. Currently teaching at Oklahoma City University and freelancing as an orchestral violinist, he also composes, arranges and records. A big part of his work is devoted to Christian music. "My students are frequent winners of violin competitions. I am teaching them how to think and feel the spirit of the music that lives in every note and without which the music is dead."

EXCELLENCE IN MUSIC